East Anglia

LANDSCAPES

John Potter

MYRIAD

LONDON

First published in 2007
by Myriad Books Limited,
35 Bishopsthorpe Road,
London SE26 4PA

Photographs and text copyright
© John Potter
John Potter has asserted his right under the
Copyright, Designs and Patents Act 1998
to be identified as the author of this work.

ISBN 1 84746 011 9
EAN 978 1 84746 011 0

Designed by Jerry Goldie Graphic Design
Printed in China

www.myriadbooks.com

Title page: the Peddars Way, the coastal path
on the north Norfolk coast;
right: Blakeney

Contents

South Lincolnshire & Norfolk

Formerly a wild wasteland of marsh and inhospitable swamps, the Fens are unique. Centred on the Wash and radiating down from south Lincolnshire, through north Norfolk towards Ely and parts of Cambridgeshire, this area of drained marshland is often called the "English Holland". The Fens were tamed by Dutch engineers in the 17th century, who created a network of intricate waterways which have developed into some of Britain's most tranquil and atmospheric landscapes.

Windmills ancient and modern

The power of the prevailing wind as it blows across East Anglia has long been harnessed for the production of energy; today, evocative traditional mills such as Heckington (left) contrast with the sleek structures of the 21st century. Gedney Marsh (above) is a new wind farm near Sutton Bridge; when fully operational there will be six turbines running 24 hours a day.

Norwich Cathedral

The county town of Norfolk, Norwich is an ecclesiastical city with over 57 medieval churches built within the city walls, 31 of which are still standing. The magnificent cathedral of the Holy and Undivided Trinity (above) dominates the city centre and is the focus of spiritual life in Norfolk. Founded in 1096 it has the second highest spire in England which soars to 315ft (96m) and makes the cathedral the most distinctive landmark in East Anglia. The roof of the nave is embellished with over one thousand carved bosses that depict biblical characters and scenes from the lives of the saints; this magnificent work of art is considered to be one of the finest treasures of medieval Europe. The cathedral is separated from the busy city streets by sturdy flint walls which protect the cathedral close (above) and create a tranquil oasis for city-dwellers and visitors.

Cathedral cloisters

The impressive two-storey cloisters, built between 1297-1430, are second only in size to those at Salisbury Cathedral. They were built to replace the original cloisters which were destroyed by fire in 1272 during riots at an annual market fair in the town. The cloisters were a key part of the original Benedictine monastery and even today there is a sense of the role the cloisters played in the monks' lives – they were the places in which the monks would read, write and teach. Doors from the cloisters led to the chapter house, the dormitory stairs, the infirmary, library, refectory and the "locutory" where the monks would talk to visitors. This last room now houses the Cathedral shop.

Norwich Castle

The castle at Norwich was originally a wooden motte and bailey construction built by William the Conqueror in 1067 to serve as his royal palace in eastern England. Over the years the castle was rebuilt but now all that exists is the central keep which was clad in Bath stone by Anthony Salvin between 1835-8. Today the castle serves as the city museum with exhibits depicting East Anglian life through the ages, from the time of Boudicca who fought the Romans, to collections of porcelain and modern British painting.

Sutton Bridge

Sutton Bridge lies at the junction of three counties – Lincolnshire, Norfolk and Cambridgeshire. Situated three miles from the Wash on the river Nene, the bridge is the gateway from south Lincolnshire to north Norfolk and Cambridgeshire. The swing bridge was manufactured and erected by A Handyside & Co Ltd of Derby and London in 1897. It is designed to allow traffic to cross but can be swung to one side when a tall ship needs to pass along the canal.

Swineshead daffodils

Lincolnshire is one of the most sparsely populated counties in England but the flat arable lands of the Fens are rich in natural resources. The soil in this region is so fertile that three crops can usually be grown in one year. Daffodil and tulip fields line the sides of the road near Swineshead in early spring, providing travellers in north Norfolk with a colourful tapestry to brighten what could sometimes seem a flat and often desolate landscape.

Castle Rising

The keep at Castle Rising is the most spectacular remnant of the massive stone structure built by William d'Aubigny around 1150 to celebrate his marriage to the widow of Henry I and his acquisition of the earldom of Sussex. The ruins of the castle are surrounded by massive earth banks and ditches and the site is an ideal spot to view the surrounding countryside and the village of Castle Rising.

Sandringham

Sandringham, the country retreat of the Queen and the Duke of Edinburgh, has been passed down through four generations of British monarchs. Situated on the north Norfolk coast, the original Georgian house was completely remodelled by 1870. Sandringham House, its museum, church and gardens are open to the public and each year thousands of visitors flock to the Sandringham Flower Show. The gardens cover 60 acres and are home to rare and historic trees, together with King George VI's garden, designed by Sir Geoffrey Jellicoe, two large lakes and a stream walk as well as Queen Alexandra's Nest, the charming summerhouse perched above Sandringham's upper lake. Rhododendrons, camellias, magnolias, azaleas, hydrangeas and fuchsias all provide spectacular displays of seasonal colour. The visitor centre and country park covers 600 acres of woodland.

Sandringham continues to be a private retreat for the royal family, although the main ground floor rooms are open to the public when the family is not in residence.

The royal family usually spend Christmas at Sandringham and remain there officially until February. The house and the surrounding area is much loved by the royal family: George V (1865-1936) wrote, "Dear old Sandringham, the place I love better than anywhere else in the world".

.

Sandringham church

The church of St Mary Magdalene (above) dates from the 16th century and is constructed, like many other west Norfolk buildings, from carstone, a reddish-brown rubble stone quarried locally. The interior of the church contains a mass of carved and painted angels, together with many royal memorials both inside and in the churchyard. The royal family traditionally attend the Christmas morning service here each year. The Queen's father, George VI, was born in York Cottage on the estate and died, aged 56, at Sandringham in February 1952. The king's coffin lay in the church watched over by the game-keepers from Sandringham before being removed to Windsor for interment.

Snettisham

South of Hunstanton on the north Norfolk coast, Snettisham is a pretty village with an RSPB nature reserve two miles to the west. The village looks across the Wash towards Lincolnshire and is one of the best places in Britain to see spectacular flocks of migrating birds on the move. In the depths of winter, at dawn and dusk, thousands of pink-footed geese commute between their safe roosts in the Wash and nearby farmland where they feed on the remnants of the sugar beet harvest. The birds make an eerie sound, not dissimilar to the rhythmic sound of a steam train as it approaches from a distance. At high tide, when the sea water covers large areas of the mudflats of the Wash, thousands of wading birds take flight and move away from their feeding grounds onto the surrounding islands and mud banks. The RSPB have provided hides from which this spectacle can be viewed. The Country Park is a popular venue for visitors with a host of attractions including a unique deer park.

Heacham

Heacham, which lies on the coast between King's Lynn
and the seaside resort of Hunstanton, has two beaches,
one to the north and one to the south. Both are ideal
locations from which to enjoy panoramic views across
the Wash. The view (right) was taken out of season in
a strong, almost gale force wind. On the eastern side
of the village is England's oldest lavender farm based at
Caley Mill. With more than 100 acres under
cultivation, the intoxicating scent of lavender drifts in
the air for miles around.

Hunstanton

"Sunny Hunny", as Hunstanton is often called, is 15 miles east of King's Lynn and has some of the best surf on the east coast of Norfolk. It is a traditional English seaside resort with many attractions, including a sea life centre, a funfair, amusement arcades, leisure centre and an aquarium. The town is rapidly becoming a centre for the sport of kite-surfing. This exciting activity is the fastest growing watersport in the world and was popularised by French and Hawaiian stars in the late 1990s.

The Old Lighthouse

Old Hunstanton, the picturesque village just east of Hunstanton, has a medieval church, two pitch and putt golf courses, a championship golf course, coastal footpaths and a nature reserve. The town's most prominent landmark is the Old Lighthouse. Beacons or lantern lights have been used to warn shipping of the dangers along this coast for centuries and the first lighthouse was built here in 1666. The present building was constructed in 1844.

Hunstanton cliffs

Close to the promenade and Beach Terrace Road lie these distinctive and eye-catching striped cliffs. This spectacular formation is a graphic display of Britain's geology over many millions of years. White chalk from the Upper Cretaceous period sits on top of a layer of limestone known as red chalk from the Lower Cretaceous period which was formed over a period of 15 million years. At the base is grey/green carstone, a coarse grainy rock often used in the past for building in this region. Fossils can be found in both the white and red chalk and it is not unusual, particularly at weekends, to find groups of fossil-hunters armed with hammers and chisels trying to prise specimens from the cliff face. The most valuable fossils, such as ammonites (large mussel shells), are to be found just after a period of stormy weather has eroded the cliff face and caused a rock fall, exposing the fossils to public gaze for the first time.

Holme next the Sea

Holme is an unspoilt coastal village, sited at the point where the 46 mile (74km) long-distance footpath known as the Peddars Way reaches its northern seaward end. The Norfolk Coastal Path that follows the coast from Hunstanton to Cromer can also be accessed here. These images, taken in winter, illustrate the beauty and remote location of this coastal area which has been designated an area of outstanding natural beauty. The shifting sand dunes are covered in marram grass which helps reduce drifting in the strong winds.

A 4,000 year-old timber circle was discovered here. Formed from oak timber posts encircling an upturned oak tree, English Heritage recorded the site and then removed the timbers for analysis.

With its square 15th-century tower, the church of St Mary is a distinctive landmark in the area. It has a simple but austere interior with three baptismal fonts, a beautiful organ and many striking memorials. The churchyard contains a number of graves of the Nelson family who lived nearby in Holme House. Admiral Horatio Nelson, a descendant of one of the sons of the family, spent his boyhood years in nearby Burnham Thorpe.

Brancaster

The Royal West Norfolk Golf Course at Brancaster is described in its brochure as being "close to the beach". This is certainly an apt description of this view seen from near the clubhouse (above) looking north at first light in January. The wide open skies, attractive unspoilt countryside and sea air make this a very popular area for golfers and there are courses at Hunstanton, Sheringham, Fakenham, King's Lynn and Castle Rising. Watersports are also catered for, with sailing and windsurfing lessons available at both Brancaster and Burnham Overy Staithe. The vast stretch of sandy beach, fringed in part by beautiful sand dunes, makes this area popular for family holidays, beach-combing and birdwatching. Brancaster alone has 2,000 acres of beach and over 4.5 miles of coastline, owned by the National Trust. The area is an important breeding ground for birds and is also the site of a Roman fort.

Chicory (*Cichorium intybus*)

Brancaster heritage

The three villages of Brancaster, Brancaster Staithe and Burnham Deepdale form a more or less continuous line along the marshland fringing Brancaster Bay. At low tide a petrified forest can be seen on the shoreline. The sheltered inlet at Brancaster Staithe was the ideal location for a harbour, and the Romans built a fort here and gave the name *Branodunum* to the area. The fort defended the coast from marauding Saxon and Frankish pirates; the garrison was manned by troops from present-day Croatia and Montenegro. Legend has it that England's greatest naval commander, Nelson, sailed his first boat at Brancaster Staithe.

Burnham

The Burnhams are a cluster of villages centred around the pretty town of Burnham Market. The area remains relatively unspoiled and it is pleasant to travel along the quiet back lanes just inland from the coast. Here the verges and hedgerows explode with summer flowers and provide excellent habitats for wildlife. This distant view of the Tower Mill at Burnham Overy Staithe is attractively framed by wild chicory plants growing along the edge of a cornfield on a sweltering summer day. This perennial herb can grow to a height of 5ft (1.5m) usually on fallow land. The pretty flowers are clustered in heads up to 1.5ins (40mm) in diameter.

Burnham sailing

Sailing is immensely popular at Burnham Overy Staithe and enthusiasts can check on the weather and tidal conditions using a webcam sited on top of the boathouse, which gives a north-easterly view of the Norfolk marshes and the sand dunes of Gun Hill. The boathouse is a traditional chandlery offering boat storage and repairs, waterproof clothing and gifts. Flagstaff House, a local self-catering holiday cottage, was once the home of Captain Woodget, master of the tea clipper *Cutty Sark*, which is now in dry dock at Greenwich in south-east London.

Holkham

Holkham Hall is a beautiful 18th-century Palladian-style country house built between 1734 and 1762 for Thomas Coke, First Earl of Leicester, on his return from his Grand Tour of Europe. The house is set in 300 acres of magnificent landscaped parkland just west of Wells-next-the-Sea and has remained substantially unchanged since its completion, with the exception of a vestibule on the north side and terraced gardens to the south, which were added during the 1850s. Among the highlights of the building are the ceiling of the spectacular 50ft high Marble Hall (mostly constructed from alabaster) which is from a design by Inigo Jones, and the opulent salon where paintings by Rubens, Van Dyke and many others are on display. The park has its own five-mile seafront and a herd of 600 fallow deer. Visitors can enjoy boat trips along the extensive lake, constructed in 1727. The unusual building (right) is a 17th-century ice house built close to the site of an earlier house, Hill Hall.

Coke of Norfolk

In 1776 the newly completed house was passed on to Thomas William Coke (1754-1842), after the death of his father. Thomas was the MP for Norfolk for over 50 years and became famous as one of Britain's greatest ever agricultural reformers. Improving the estate at Holkham was, for him, the passion of a lifetime and he was the instigator of the Holkham "shearings", which were the forerunner of today's agricultural shows. People flocked from Britain and overseas to the shearings to learn more about his methods of animal husbandry. It was largely due to Coke that the agricultural revolution of the early 19th century took place.

Wells-next-the-Sea

One of the most attractive towns of the north Norfolk coast, and a busy harbour, Wells-next-the-Sea is a charming, historic seaside resort brimming with character and atmosphere. Despite its name, the town now stands about a mile from open water. It is packed with historic houses and narrow lanes, or "yards", lead down to the bustling quayside. At low tide the beach seems to stretch to the far horizon and there are striking views to the west towards Holkham and Burnham Overy Staithe. The inland saltmarshes are a haven for wildlife and very popular with birdwatchers. A popular attraction for children is the tradition of "gillying" (fishing) for crabs around the quay. The historic Dutch sailing boat *The Albatross*, one of the oldest sailing ships still afloat, is often moored at the quay. The beach (left) is within easy reach of the Holkham Nature reserve. The beautiful beach huts are sited close to a stretch of pine woodland beside a long sweeping beach, half a mile from the quay.

Blakeney

The National Trust acquired the area around Blakeney Point in 1912 and established it as the first nature reserve in Norfolk; most of the area is open to the public. Covering 2,400 acres, the protected conservation area includes the long sand and shingle spit of Blakeney Point as well as marshes at Morston and Cley. It is one of Britain's foremost bird sanctuaries and is a natural habitat for migratory birds, some of which are unique to this area. Important species include shelduck, oystercatchers, ringed plovers and little, common,

Sandwich and Arctic tern, who nest here on the shingle ridges following over-wintering in Africa.

Blakeney Point is also famous for its grey and common seal colonies. There are approximately 500 seals in this mixed colony and boats are able to get remarkably close to the seals without seeming to disturb their normal sleepy demeanour. The best way to see the seals is to join a boat trip from either Blakeney or Morston Quays. Some trips include a stop and short walk on Blakeney Point itself.

Cley-next-the-Sea

The Norfolk coast is renowned for its attractive villages constructed from flint and Cley is arguably one of the finest. The village is sited midway between Wells-next-the-Sea and Cromer. In its early years, Cley had a reputation as a centre of piracy and smuggling and it was not until 1673 when a local landowner, Sir Henry Calthorpe, started to drain the marshes that the area began to lose its lawless reputation and trade developed along the wharves and warehouses close to Cley windmill. Soon Cley became one of the busiest ports in Britain trading in fish, cloths, spices, coal and cereal crops, mostly with the Low Countries. Cley is steeped in history as visitors can discover if they take the village trail which goes past the old village forge, the former smokehouse and the post office, which was used as a troop billet in the first world war. Cley windmill, one of the best-loved landmarks in the area, dates from the early 18th century. It overlooks the saltmarshes, Cley bird sanctuary and the sea.

Salthouse Marshes

Salthouse Marshes, seen here at dusk, are one of a string of important birding sites along the north Norfolk coast. The area contains a number of fresh and saltwater lagoons, protected to the north by a long and high shingle bank and fringed by marshland to the south. This habitat is ideal for wildlife and particularly for birds. As its name suggests, the village of Salthouse and the nearby marshes were once a centre for salt production. The village was largely made up of warehouses for the storage of salt. The village was inundated during the spring flood of 1953 and many of the old buildings were lost. Traditions die hard in this region and managing and cutting gorse to feed the bakehouse is still remembered by some of the elderly residents.

Salthouse

The village of Salthouse is still a magical place steeped in history and tradition. The settlement is made up of a scattering of flint cottages, a post office, an inn and a seafood restaurant. The church of St Nicholas stands in an imposing position overlooking the village and the marshes beyond. It is reached by a track from the shore, lined with flint walls and was built in this lofty position in the 16th century by Sir Henry Heydon to protect it from flooding and to act as a beacon for ships out at sea.

The church has beautiful stained-glass windows and, on the choir stalls, graffiti can be seen which dates from the 18th century and depicts the tall-masted sailing ships of the times.

Cookie's Crab Shop (left) has been selling high-quality shellfish for over three generations and their delicious fish can be enjoyed in the garden overlooking the saltmarshes.

Weybourne Mill

The five-storey redbrick and flint tower of Weybourne Mill with its white boat-shaped cap, pantiled roof and sails is a picture-book example of a Norfolk windmill. It occupies a prominent position on the east side of the village. The mill was built in 1850 and has been restored twice, once in the 1920s and more recently in the late 1960s. Corn was last ground here during the first world war when the mill was used as a watchtower by the military. When in use it was fed by Spring Beck which rises in woods near Weybourne railway station about one mile away. A mill pond was constructed to control the flow of water. In 2006 all the machinery with the exception of the turbine was removed and the mill is now in residential use.

Sheringham

Fishing was once the lifeblood of this attractive town and even today at sunrise fishermen continue to push their boats out to sea from the gap in the cliffs known as "The Hythe", while holidaymakers are still fast asleep dreaming of sunshine, sandy beaches and crab sandwiches. The fishermen store their boats and equipment as their forebears did between Westcliff and the Fishermen's Slope close to the lifeboat shed. In the late 19th century Sheringham boasted over 150 fishing boats; the way of life of this close-knit fishing community is well-documented in the local museum. Born and bred Sheringham people are termed "Shannocks" and the nicknames of some of the fishermen – Butter Balls, Bread-Alone, Pongo and Teapot – bear testimony to the rich community life enjoyed by the residents of old. Now tourism, which began with the arrival of the railway in 1887, supports the majority of the local community. But the character of the town is nurtured by the Sheringham and District Local Preservation Society, who are in the process of restoring the fishing sheds between Westcliff and the Fishermen's Slope.

West Runton

West Runton is a quiet village situated between Sheringham and Cromer. It benefits from being a stop on the picturesque Bittern railway line which links Norwich with the north Norfolk coastal towns of Cromer and Sheringham. The town sits high on the top of the cliffs at Cromer Ridge, which runs from Cromer to Holt. Holidaymakers love the safe sandy beach (below) and a favourite summer pastime is to comb the rockpools and low cliffs searching for sea life and fossils. A local attraction is the Shire Horse Centre which has a wonderful collection of these beautiful animals with the agricultural machinery they powered in the recent past.

The village sensationally hit the headlines in 1995, when the well-preserved skeleton of a mammoth – the "West Runton Elephant"– was excavated from the cliffs. Just behind the village the National Trust has acquired an area of woodland and heath where there was once a Roman camp. At 328ft (100m) above sea level this is the highest point in Norfolk.

Cromer

Cromer parish church dominates this beautiful and elegant seaside resort. Its spire is 160ft (50m) high; climbing the 172 steps to the top provides visitors with breathtaking views of the town and out to the North Sea. From this lofty perch they can contemplate the fate of the village of Shipden which was swallowed up by the sea during the middle ages; Shipden's church is now reckoned to be at least 437 yards (400m) from the shoreline – a warning if one were needed that coastal erosion is certainly not a recent problem along the Norfolk coast.

The magnificent midsummer sunrise (below), with the whole of the seafront bathed in gentle warm sunshine, is an invitation to sit on one of the benches for a while and enjoy the view. Cromer's expansion as a seaside resort was hastened in the late Victorian era when a rail link from Norwich and the Midlands led to the construction of many grand hotels. In 1887 the town was so popular that a second railway station, Cromer Beach (now Cromer station), was built close to the seafront. The town was a favourite with wealthy families from Norwich who built summer homes here.

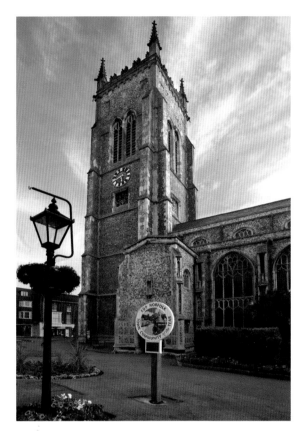

Cromer pier

Piers and jetties have long been a feature of Cromer life: in 1390, Richard III decreed that the town should be allowed to levy taxes on incoming cargo to pay for a landing stage and pier. In the 19th century two wooden jetties graced the shoreline – the first, built in 1822, was wrecked by a storm and replaced by a second which was destroyed in 1897 when a coal boat collided with the structure. The current elegant Edwardian pier celebrated its centenary in 2001 and was one of the first "pleasure" piers constructed in the 20th century. A great attraction for visitors, the 510-seat Pavilion Theatre provides a traditional end-of-pier "Seaside Special" show throughout the summer season. In 2000 Cromer pier was winner of the "Pier of the Year" award. Competing with the pier as Cromer's best-loved attraction is the Cromer crab, the town's famous culinary delicacy which has been harvested by local fishermen for centuries. Regarded by afficionados as the "king of British crabs", it is the basic ingredient of many local recipes.

Cromer fishing

Sea fishing with rods is extremely popular all along the north Norfolk coast. Some fish from the beach, casting into the surf from the edge of the seashore. Others charter boats from Blakeney, Cromer or Sheringham and go deep-sea fishing. Fly fishing is available at Bure Valley Lakes and coarse fishing on the Broads, lakes and rivers in the region. At Cromer the prime spot from which to fish is the third breakwater east of the pier, where the water is deepest, and the last three hours of a high tide generally yields a good catch. In late autumn and winter cod and codling can be caught at high tide beyond the promenade from the West Beach.

Happisburgh

Happisburgh (pronounced "Haisburgh" or "Hazeburgh") is a pretty seaside village whose distinctive lighthouse is a dominant and much-loved landmark in the area around Sea Palling and Mundesley. Built in 1791, it is Britain's only private working lighthouse and is the oldest lighthouse on the Norfolk coast. In 1990 the 85ft (26m) tall building was threatened with closure but was saved by the Happisburgh Lighthouse Trust who now run and maintain the structure.

This coastline has always been a dangerous place for shipping and a visit to the graveyard at the local church of St Mary reveals evidence of many tragedies, including a mass grave commemorating the lives of 119 seamen from *HMS Invincible*. Their ship came aground on the notorious Happisburgh Sands in 1801, when the vessel was travelling to join Nelson's fleet at the Battle of Copenhagen.

Coastal erosion

During the last few decades the wooden sea defences built to protect Happisburgh have been failing and large sections of the sandy cliffs regularly fall into the sea. On the night of January 31 1953 a great flood caused by an exceptionally high spring tide claimed the lives of 76 Norfolk people, flooded thousands of homes and carried away houses and shops in Happisburgh. The village regularly features on local and international news as the sea advances closer and closer. The local population are now at the forefront of a campaign to persuade the Government not to abandon sea defences in a new policy of "managed retreat". This race against time is critical in many ways: according to archaeologists Happisburgh is a key site and the crumbling coastline around the village may well yield further discoveries about Britain's earliest human inhabitants.

The Broads

The large water-filled Broads (lakes) are connected by over 200 miles of navigable rivers, dykes and cuts. Although this watery region straddles both Norfolk and Suffolk it is known as the Norfolk Broads. There are over 50 Broads but only 13 of them are usually open to the fleets of pleasurecraft which ply these waterways, particularly in the summer. The Broads are managed by the Broads Authority and certain areas have been given conservation status, rather like a national park. Hickling Broad, fringed by vast drifts of reedbeds, teems with rare wildlife, including swallowtail butterflies, bitterns, heron, bearded tits in summer, and many protected plants.

Hickling boathouses

Hickling Broad is the largest of the navigable lakes in the Broads, covering over 14,000 acres. The moorings at Hickling Broad by the Pleasure Boat Inn are a very popular port of call and the pretty and secluded village of Hickling is just a stroll away. The nature reserve here is maintained by the Norfolk Wildlife Trust. These thatched boathouses were photographed early in February on a bitterly cold morning following a light frost.

Horsey

Horsey Mill, a fully restored drainage windpump, has been owned by the National Trust since 1948. It was entirely rebuilt in 1912, and stands proudly beside the edge of Horsey Mere between Sea Palling and Winterton-on-Sea. The redbrick building has five storeys and from the top visitors can enjoy superb views of the Broads and coast. In 1961 the mill was restored but had its "tail" blown off in the great October hurricane of 1987 – not the first time in its history that this had happened. Mills in this part of the country have had a varied history. They have often been used as a convenient hiding place for contraband by local smugglers. At other periods – particularly during times of war – they have been drafted into service as lookout towers.

Martham

This beautiful area is on the edge of the Broads National Park, nine miles north of Great Yarmouth. Saxons settled here around AD600 and named the village "the ham of martens" (the home of the polecats); these cream-coloured, ferret-like animals were common in Broadland marshes until the early 20th century.

Martham borders the southern bank of the river Thurne, one of the popular highways for boating traffic. Just north of the village lies Martham Broad, the centre of the 140 acre reserve maintained by English Nature.

Martham Broad

The National Nature Reserve at Martham Broad is managed by the Norfolk Wildlife Trust. It can be approached on foot from the staithe (mooring) at West Somerton and contains rare species such as the swallowtail butterfly and marsh harrier. The heron (left), nature's most accomplished fisherman, was photographed soon after sunrise basking in the early warm sunshine.

In the early middle ages the village of Martham grew to a sizeable settlement of over 1,000 inhabitants due to the fact that its local landowner, the bishop of Thetford, Herbert de Losingo built the cathedral at Norwich and was a patron of the monastery there. The inhabitants of Martham earned a living supplying the monks with food and fuel. Later, from the 17th century, brickmaking became an important activity; many of the older houses in the village feature the famous "Norfolk red bricks" which all have the same appearance, texture and colour. Today, the picture-postcard village with its duckpond is surrounded by pretty houses, many of them thatched.

East Somerton

Blood Hill wind farm is located to the east of Winterton-on-Sea on either side of a minor road that runs from East Somerton towards Gibbet Hill. The 10 turbines were constructed in 1992 as one of the first wind farms in Britain. They generate enough power to supply around 1,000 homes. This image was taken just after sunrise. The names Blood Hill and Gibbet Hill are a reminder of the area's violent history – a battle took place here between Saxons and Vikings reputedly so terrible that the hills ran red with blood.

West Somerton

Boats can moor in the dyke at West Somerton, where there is a post office store and the Lion Inn is just five minutes walk from the village staithe. Robert Hales, known as "the Norfolk giant", is buried on the south side of the village church. He was 7ft 8ins and weighed over 32 stone; he appeared at fairs and shows throughtout England.

The area around the Somertons is a patchwork of gently rolling hills, old traditional windmills, church spires and wind pumps. Visitors can often enjoy the tranquil sight of ships' sails drifting across wide horizons. From the dyke, boats can access the river Thurne which rises close to Martham Broad and then flows for around six miles to Thurne Mouth where it joins the Bure.

How Hill

How Hill on the river Ant is close to the Broadland village of Ludham. Nearby is How Hill House, a magnificent thatched Arts & Crafts country house, famous for its Edwardian gardens and views over the surrounding marshes. The architect Edward Boardman built it as a summer house for his family in 1904 and it became a study centre in 1967. It is surrounded by a 365 acre estate which contains the delightful Toad Hole Cottage Museum. Located in an original marshman's cottage this gives visitors a fascinating insight into Victorian life on the Broads.

There are three restored windmills at How Hill. The wind pump (left) is typical of the skeletal structures that punctuate the skyline in so many areas of East Anglia. Nearby is the evocative Turf Fen windmill (far left).

The entire estate is a microscosm of Broads life and its unique habitat. The area consists of open fen, wet and dry woodland, fen meadows, rush pastures and two areas of open water. Windmills, evening skies and still water are irresistible to artists and photographers, and inquisitive swans can almost be guaranteed to approach when they see someone by the water's edge.

Thurne

The river Thurne begins at the junction of the river Bure and runs to West Somerton – a popular stretch of river for boats cruising the Norfolk Broads. Thurne Mill is one of the most photographed locations on the Broads. It is a very tall, white, elegant mill standing on the east bank of the river. It is open to the public during weekends and access to the top, via a very steep ladder, gives excellent views of the surrounding fens and marshes. The mill houses a small exhibition and is owned by the Norfolk Windmill Trust. Adjacent to the windmill, Thurne Dyke gives access to the village and the local inn, The Lion.

On the opposite bank stands St Benet's Level windpump. Close by Thurne village is the beautiful 13th-century church of St Edmunds which looks out towards the romantic ruin of the 10th-century St Benet's Abbey.

Reed-cutting

The extensive reedbeds of the Broads have traditionally supplied thatching material for local houses, and to make windbreaks and fences. Harvesting of the reeds takes place between December and April. In the past, the reed-cutting industry supplied much needed income during the winter when fishing was difficult and work on the land was scarce. Today most of the reeds are cut mechanically but in sensitive areas hand-cutting is still used. The reeds are raked by hand to clean out old vegetation and then tied into tight bundles with twine. In the summer, reedcutters are employed to cut the sedge which is used for dressing the top of thatched roofs. Reed-cutting is vital since it helps to preserve the important wildlife of the Broads and the coast. It is a sustainable industry which employs local labour.

Upton Staithe

The small village of Upton is situated west of Great Yarmouth on the northern edge of the Broads. Upton Staithe (above) has good cruiser moorings. At low tide the dyke is shallow and it is tricky for boating enthusiasts to navigate between the lines of moored yachts. The village contains the attractive church of St Margaret and a local pub – the White Horse Inn. Near Upton Broad, Upton Fen is managed by the Norfolk Wildlife Trust.

St Olaves

A few miles south-west of Great Yarmouth lies St Olaves and its near neighbour Herringfleet. The area is the site of three mills: St Olaves Drainage Mill (left) seen here on the east bank of the river Waveney looking up the river from St Olaves Bridge; Mallets Mill which drained the Scales Marshes and was demolished in 1893; and the Smock Drainage Mill which stands a mile south-west of the Norman church of Herringfleet. St Olaves Mill was built around 1910 by Dan England, the Ludham millwright. It also drives a scoop wheel for lifting marsh water from the ditches.

Mill workings

In the heart of rural Norfolk, north-east of King's Lynn, Bircham Mill is a beautifully restored and fully working windmill. In the 19th century there were around 300 mills grinding corn for horsefeed and breadmaking in Norfolk alone. Bircham is now the only mill in working order in the region that is open to the public. It has five floors and on windy days visitors can enjoy watching the sails turning and the machinery working. There are many items connected with the miller's trade on display in the tea rooms, bakery and grounds. The windmill was built in 1846 and survived until the 1920s when the sails were removed and the tower was abandoned. Panoramic views of the surrounding countryside can be enjoyed from the fifth storey fan deck and a pictorial history of the windmill's restoration is on display in the stable room.

A major attraction at the mill is the smell of freshly-baked bread. The original 200-year-old oven is still here; when in use it could bake 100 loaves simultaneously. In the past local people walked several miles to buy their bread. Ponies are still kept here – a reminder of the time when horse and cart were the only means of delivering materials to and from the busy mill.

Houghton Hall

This fine Palladian mansion was built by Sir Robert Walpole between 1722-1735. He was Britain's first prime minister and served in the reign of George I and George II. The architects were Colen Campbell and James Gibbs. The house was built by Thomas Ripley, and the huge and imposing stable block by William Kent who also supervised the elaborate and ornate interior decorations.

Houghton village was first mentioned in the Domesday book in 1086; the medieval St Martin's church in the grounds of Houghton Hall was begun a century later in the Early English style and completed in 1271. The Walpoles – a landowning family from the villages of Walpole St Peter and Walpole Cross Keys, just west of King's Lynn – came to the area as lords of the manor in 1307.

Parkland

Houghton Hall is set in 350 acres of fine parkland and gardens. A large herd of rare white fallow deer roam freely, together with small groups of "exotic" deer. An unusual feature of the house is its Toy Soldier Museum. This was established by the 6th Marquess, Lord Cholmondley, who was awarded the Military Cross for valour during the Second World War. It consists of over 20,000 model soldiers and large scenes of the Battle of Waterloo and other famous conflicts. There is also a newly restored five-acre walled garden which is divided into separate garden "rooms" with sections for fruit and vegetables, a croquet lawn and glass house.

The unusual tower cupola (left) complete with weather vane and sundials is mounted above one of the twin side buildings on either side of the main house.

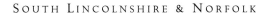

Little Walsingham

Little Walsingham has been a place of religious pilgrimage since the 11th century when a vision of the Virgin Mary appeared to a local noblewoman. It is often described as "England's Nazareth". Over the years, millions of pilgrims have followed the procession from the parish church of St Mary (left) to the Abbey grounds where the shrine of Our Lady of Walsingham is housed. They traditionally walk the mile and a half to the Slipper Chapel where pilgrims leave their shoes before walking on to the Holy House.

St Mary's is a magnificent building. The interior of the church is spacious and lavishly decorated. The superb Seven Sacrament octagonal font, common in East Anglian churches, has been exquisitely crafted. It is held in such high regard that a plaster replica was taken to the Great Exhibition of 1851.

The quaint streets in the village of Little Walsingham are full of medieval and Georgian houses. The old weathered door (below) is to be found on the medieval water pump in the centre of the village.

Blickling Hall

One of England's finest Jacobean houses, famous for its long gallery, fine furniture, superb library, pictures and tapestries, Blickling Hall is a short distance north-west of Aylsham. The house was built on the site of a former manor house and was once home to Anne Boleyn, the wife of Henry VIII and the mother of Elizabeth I. Legend has it that her ghost haunts the house. Today, Blickling, which is surrounded by stunning scenery and parkland, is owned by the National Trust; it was first opened to the public in 1962. The gardens consist of three separate areas – the Jacobean Garden, the Georgian Garden and the Lothian Garden, named after the eighth Marquess of Lothian and his wife Constance. The house was requisitioned during the second world war and used as the officers mess for nearby RAF Oulton.

Castle Acre and Priory

A few miles north of Swaffham on the Fakenham road, Castle Acre is an attractive small town perched high up within the outer bailey of a castle. The defensive earthworks are dramatic – the inner bailey covers 15 acres and the motte is over 100ft (30m) high. The impressive and ornate Bailey Gate stands to this day and separates the castle from the village where there are some pretty cottages, several inns, a craft shop, village store and a tea room.

The impressive ruins of the Cluniac Priory (right) are a 10-minute stroll down a quiet secluded lane just south of the village. The well-preserved west front of the priory is one of the finest in England and a good indicator of its standing in the region when it was first built. The Cluniac Order (from Cluny in France) was founded in AD 909 and over time became extremely wealthy and somewhat removed from their original vows of simplicity and poverty. The priory eventually suffered from debts and scandals in the 13th and 14th centuries and finally the monks were arrested in 1351 when they were no more than vagabonds. Today the village is a major tourist attraction in Norfolk.

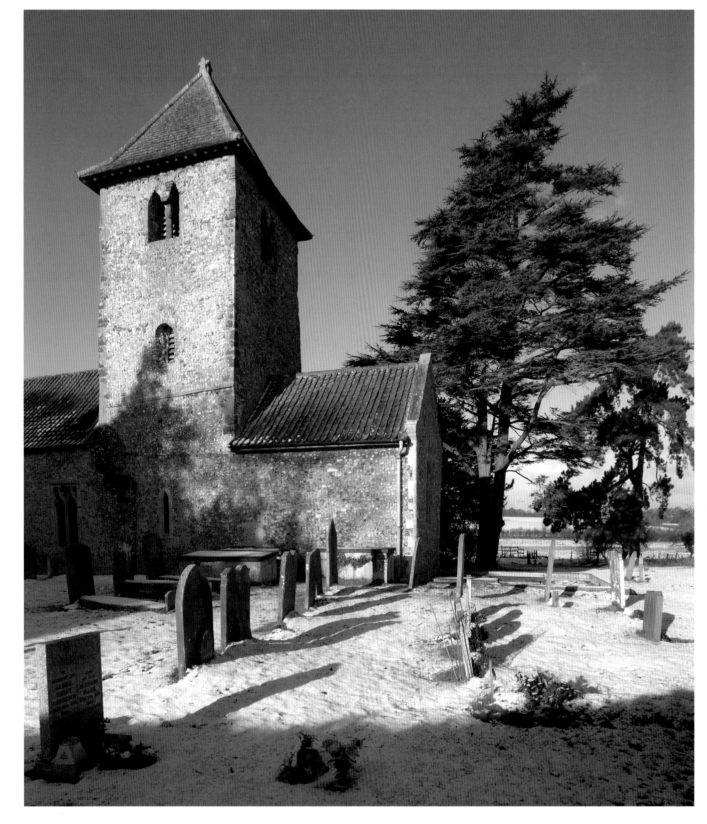

Newton All Saints

This attractive rustic church stands in the village of Newton, which is just west of Castle Acre on the A1065. It has a sturdy Saxon tower with a tiled roof and almost looks Tuscan. The church was photographed in February after a fine dusting of snow. Some of the interior brickwork is reputed to be Roman in origin. The church was originally built in the shape of a cross but the builldings which made up the "arms" of the cross were demolished in the 18th century, leaving a simple nave. The rubble outlines of these demolished structures can still be seen.

Swaffham

The picturesque market town of Swaffham, which lies midway between Downham Market and Dereham, was a very wealthy town and the home of many important members of the aristocracy in the 18th century. In the centre of the town is the newly refurbished and spacious marketplace, several elegant Georgian buildings, a domed rotunda and the 15th-century church of St Peter and St Paul, which is one of the finest in the area. It has one of the best double hammerbeam roofs in England and is built of Barnack stone and flint. Two notable monuments are to be found in the church – one to John Botewright, chaplain to Henry VI, and one to Katherine Steward, Oliver Cromwell's grandmother.

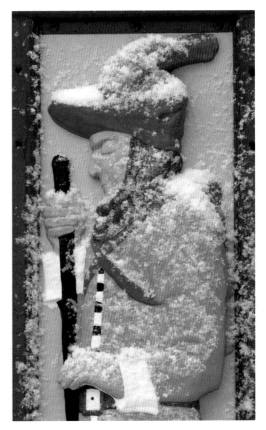

Pedlar of Swaffham

The town sign (above) depicts the legend of the Pedlar of Swaffham. The pedlar dreamed that if he stood on London Bridge his fortune would be made. He travelled to London but after spending three days and nights on the bridge was dismayed to find that his dream had come to nothing. Eventually, a local shopkeeper spotted the pedlar who told him his story. The shopkeeper burst into amazed laughter – only the night before the shopkeeper dreamed that a huge chest of money lay beneath a pedlar's house in Swaffham! The pedlar quickly returned home and unearthed the treasure, hidden just where the shopkeeper had predicted.

Cambridgeshire and Suffolk

The countryside around Cambridge is an area of wide open skies and flat fenland, divided into a patchwork of large fields. This intensively farmed landscape is punctuated by slow-moving rivers, water meadows and pretty villages whose church steeples peep out above the surrounding countryside. Neighbouring Suffolk is home to miles of unspoilt coastline around Aldeburgh and Southwold. In south Suffolk a large area of coast and heathland, stretching from the northern side of the Stour estuary to the eastern fringes of Ipswich, has been designated an area of outstanding natural beauty. The area includes farmland, ancient woodland, heathland, reedbeds, estuaries, grazing marsh, commercial forestry, crumbling cliffs and wonderful shingle beaches.

Cambridge

The county town and home of the famous university, Cambridge is one of the busiest tourist spots in Britain. But the city still manages to retain the air of a bustling market town thanks to its narrow streets and the green meadows which extend into the heart of the college area. The sight of punts on the river Cam, glorious college architecture, May balls and cyclists all help to give Cambridge a romantic air that is almost unique amongst British cities.

The university

The city centre is dominated by many of the university's historic buildings. Cambridge is the second oldest university in the English-speaking world. The School of Pythagoras, one of the first educational establishments in Cambridge, was founded in 1200, and the building still stands in the grounds of St John's College. King's College (left) was founded in 1441 by Henry VI. It is a superb example of Gothic architecture and its famous chapel is home to the renowned King's College choir, whose Christmas Eve service is broadcast around the world. Clare College (below) is the second oldest of the Cambridge colleges, and was founded in 1326. It has an enviable, idyllic and peaceful location with extensive riverside gardens. The gardens form part of the famous Backs – the rear part of those colleges which border the river Cam.

Cambridge city life

The centre of Cambridge is packed with historic buildings, many of which are part of the university. But Cambridge is more than a university town – and the town centre is full of the hustle and bustle of everyday life. The Baron of Beef pub (above), in Bridge Street, a short walk from Magdalene Bridge, is one of the most historic pubs in the city. It first opened in 1752 and its distinctive name refers to a "large, double slice of beef".

Cambridge's busy market takes place in front of the University Church commonly known as Great St Mary which dominates Market Hill. A climb up the tower is a major highlight of any visit to the city. There has been a church on this site since the early 13th century and the building was used for annual ceremonies, such as the conferment of degrees, until the Senate House was built in 1730. The church clock was installed in 1793 and shortly afterwards two Cambridge undergraduates composed its chime, subsequently used by Big Ben in London and famous the world over as the "Westminster chime".

The market is open every day for general produce and plants; on Sunday there is an art and craft and farmers' market.

River and meadowland

No visit to Cambridge is complete without a trip in a punt along the river Cam. These traditional flat-bottomed boats were used widely in the Fens, the marshy flatlands north of the city and were introduced as pleasurecraft to the town in Edwardian times. You can hire a boat and try your hand at punting – it's not as easy as it looks! – or you can join a party and lie back and enjoy the splendid views.

Cambridge is famous for its beautiful meadowland which extends into the heart of the city. Trumpington Meadows (above) are close to the University Botanical Gardens with their superb displays of fenland plants.

Grantchester

A favourite walk from Newnham on the south-west side of Cambridge is to follow the path along the river Cam upstream for approximately two miles until you reach the open countryside of the famous Grantchester Meadows which extend on both sides of the river. A little further on you reach the village of Grantchester itself, its famous Orchard Tea Gardens and the old village mill pond (below).

Orchard Tea Garden

The famous Orchard Tea Garden (left) and the adjoining Old Vicarage will forever be associated with the Cambridge poet Rupert Brooke (1887-1915). As an undergraduate, Brooke would often walk with friends to Grantchester and visit Mrs Stevenson of Orchard House who had a small business serving refreshments to visitors beneath the fruit trees at the rear of her home. These trips made such an impression on the young Brooke that after leaving Cambridge he moved to the Old Vicarage next door to the Orchard.

Over the next few years, Brooke's reputation as a poet grew and he found himself at the centre of a literary circle known as the Grantchester Group. Brooke died at the early age of 27 of blood poisoning on the way to fight at the Battle of Gallipoli.
His statue (above) now stands in front of the Old Vicarage. Brooke's poem, *The Old Vicarage, Grantchester* referring to the tea room and the church of St Andrew and St Mary in the village ends with these words:

Stands the church clock at ten to three?
And is there honey still for tea?

St Neots

The largest town in Cambridgeshire, St Neots is situated on the Great Ouse, which meanders peacefully through the town and forms the border with the historic county of Huntingdonshire. The town owes its development to both God and Mammon. It was the site of a medieval priory built to house the remains of the Cornish monk, Neot, who had been canonised for his work in helping the poor; his bones were brought to the settlement in order to attract pilgrims and a market developed.

The growing town received its market charter in 1130 and continued to flourish but the priory did not survive Dissolution. Today the tower of the parish church of St Mary, known as the "cathedral of Huntingdonshire" dominates St Neots which regularly plays host to an enticing French market. The mosaic to St Neot is at the heart of the market square.

Ely Cathedral

The city of Ely is an elegant local centre dominated by its cathedral which is known locally as the "ship of the Fens" because of its slender tower which looms above the surrounding flat countryside. The cathedral is a remarkable example of Romanesque architecture and "the Octagon", an eight-sided tower in the centre of the church (below right), is the only Gothic dome in existence. The cathedral was completed in 1189 and is set within the walls of a Benedictine monastery. Today the cathedral is particularly famous for its choir and organ music.

Ely attractions

The Stained Glass Musuem is housed in the south transept of the cathedral. This magnificent collection has works of art from 1,300 years of British glass manufacture and includes works by Raphael, William Morris and John Piper.

In the shadow of the cathedral is Oliver Cromwell's house, the only remaining home other than Hampton Court where he and his family are known to have lived.

The Maltings Quayside area, sited on the banks of the Great River Ouse (above right) has been redeveloped from a brewery which dates from 1868. This stretch of river is used by the Cambridge University crew to practise every year for the famous Oxford and Cambridge Boat Race.

The Quayside

Until the draining of the Fens in the 17th century, Ely was an island. It is now situated on the Great Ouse and, until the 18th century, was a significant port until the arrival of the railways. The town is now popular with boating enthusiasts and has a large marina. The Quayside has been beautifully restored with inns and restaurants and visitors can take a trip in a narrowboat to Cambridge. The picturesque Prickwillow Engine House is located on the river Lark to the north-east.

81

Thelnetham Windmill

This fully working windmill lies on the edge of the village of Thelnetham, between Diss and Thetford. Beautifully restored, it is an early 19th-century tower mill and can be visited by appointment. It is close to the source of two rivers, the Waveney and the Little Ouse, and nearby footpaths lead on to Knettishall Heath and Thetford town centre. The windmill is also handy for the White Horse Inn, the village pub and restaurant. Thelnetham has strong literary associations – the writer John Middleton Murry, who was married to Katherine Mansfield, was a famous resident, in the 1940s. He purchased the old village school for local people to use as a village hall.

Knettishall

The wild heathland (left) at Knettishall Heath is typical of the beautiful landscape in this area and is the result of centuries of past human activity. Today, Knettishall Country Park and the surrounding heathland – known as "the Brecks" – is very popular with walkers and wildlife enthusiasts. The park is a hub for a number of long-distance footpaths, including the Angles Way, which links the Brecks to the Norfolk Broads, the Icknield Way, which dates from around 4000BC, is 120 miles long and finishes in Buckinghamshire, and the 95-mile Peddars Way which passes through the heath, and follows a Roman road to the north Norfolk Coast.

The Roman military road was built at the time of the Boudiccan revolt in AD61, possibly in order to enable troops to patrol the territory of the troublesome and unruly Iceni tribe. The word "peddars" is a corruption of "pedlars", the travelling sales reps of the past. The Peddars Way first appeared on maps around 1587, and could also mean footpath from the Latin *pedester* – "to go on foot".

Billingford Mill

Close to the Norfolk border and the river Waveney, the Billingford tower cornmill stands near the Diss to Harleston road. It was built by W Skinner between 1859 and 1860 to replace a post mill which had been destroyed in a gale. The redbrick tower mill cost £1,300 to build and has five storeys. Originally the boat-shaped cap was tarred, but is now painted white. It has an unusual six-blade fantail, and is a very prominent landmark. It is the last mill in Norfolk to be worked by wind, and in 1997 considerable restoration work was undertaken by the

NORFOLK

BILLINGFORD MILL

A typical brick tower mill complete with Norfolk boatshape cap, fantail and sails. Built in 1860 by George Goddard to replace an earlier post mill; it was the last working mill in Norfolk until 1956. Purchased by Victor Valiant for preservation it was given to the Norfolk Windmills Trust and subsequently restored.

WINDMILLS TRUST

Norfolk Windmills Trust. Close by is the Old Post Office which has now been fully restored as miller's accommodation, and there are plans to develop the smithy garden as a natural herb garden and teashop. The remarkable tree sculpture (right) is one of several works of rural art located in fields near the county border.

84

Barsham flower festival

Suffolk has more medieval churches than any other county in England – there were more than 400 at the time of the Domesday Book in 1088. The village of Barsham is situated on the road from Bungay to Beccles and Holy Trinity Church, across a meadow from the road, has a long tradition of flower festivals. Nearby Bungay has both a district horticultural society and a flower club, so the area is renowned for its magnificent gardens. Holy Trinity is one of Suffolk's great Anglo-Catholic shrines, and for centuries visitors have journeyed here to visit and worship. A notable feature of this ancient building is the extraordinary flint lattice that spreads across the face of the east wall.

Southwold

Southwold, a unique and elegant seaside town, has an atmosphere and charm that is quintessentially English. A favourite holiday destination for thousands of visitors each year, the town and surrounding district have many attractions. Bounded by the North Sea to the east, the river Blyth and Southwold harbour to the south-west, and Buss Creek to the north, Southwold is virtually an island. The surrounding countryside is picturesque with many pretty villages. The river Blyth estuary is popular for boating, with its reed beds and saltings, woodlands, open heaths and gently rolling farmland. Fishing was the town's main industry for over 900 years, with herring being particularly important. In the past catches were so good that there was a tithe levied on fish to be paid to the local parish. Southwold's maritime history is preserved at the Sailor's Reading Room, one of the town's four splendid museums. To the north of the High Street lies the church of St Edmund (right), one of Suffolk's grandest churches.

86

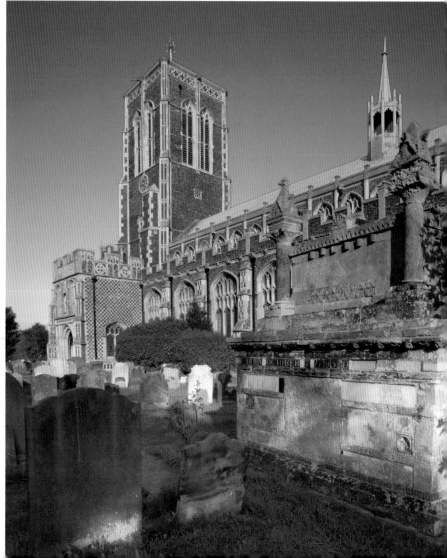

Local brewery

In 1872 George and Ernest Adnams bought the Sole Bay Brewery in Southwold and established Adnams, now one of the major businesses in the town. Adnams has many pubs in East Anglia and two fine hotels in Southwold, the Swan and the Crown. The firm uses dray horses to deliver beer locally.

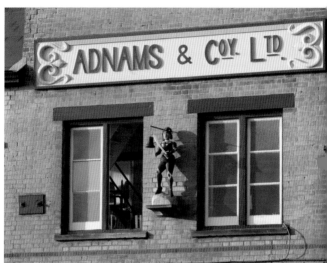

Southwold attractions

The resort has over 300 beautifully painted beach huts which evolved from fishermen's and bathers' huts. Today they are much sought after, and change hands for high sums. The huts are lifted from the beach each autumn by a giant crane in order to be safe from high tides. The tall white tower of the lighthouse (right) is a notable landmark in the centre of the town; constructed in 1887 it replaced three local lighthouses threatened by coastal erosion.

Blythburgh

Surrounded by beautiful countryside, Blythburgh is a small village four miles from the North Sea at Southwold. With a tidal river, heathland, marshes and woods, the area is a magnet for wildlife enthusiasts and birdwatchers.

The village is famous for its magnificent parish church, the Holy Trinity, which towers over the estuary. Known as "The Cathedral of The Marshes" it is part of a religious tradition in the area dating back to the first century. Over the years the church has suffered from a series of disasters, both man-made and natural. The steeple has been struck by lightning, the interior was damaged by Puritans during the Civil War, and for long periods the church was neglected. Now beautifully restored, it is often used as a venue for concerts during the Aldeburgh Summer Festival.

88

The marshes

This photograph of Blythburgh marshes shortly after sunrise appears almost monochrome, and captures the distinct character of the Suffolk coastal estuaries. The marshes around the town are at the heart of a Site of Special Scientific Interest and are internationally important for wildlife, in particular for wintering waders and wildfowl. They are often fringed by saltmarsh plants that adapt to the conditions. Birds most commonly seen here include redshank, lapwing, knot, curlew, dunlin, avocet, grey plover, golden plover, marsh harrier and shelducks.

Walberswick

Just across the river Blyth from Southwold, Walberswick was once a thriving trading port dealing in fish, bacon, cheese, corn and timber. The town's prosperity is reflected in the magnificent St Andrews church (below right) which stands at the top of the village. Today Walberswick is a popular destination with an attractive harbour and a village green surrounded by quaint houses. A ferryboat across the river links the town with Southwold to the north. To the south lie the wooded heaths of Dunwich and the Minsmere Bird Sanctuary. The resort is famous for hosting the British Open Crabbing Championships each year when hundreds of competitors try to haul as many crabs as they can from the waters of the estuary. Over the years Walberswick has attracted many artists, including Wilson Steer and Charles Rennie Mackintosh.

Dunwich

Once the capital of East Anglia, Dunwich was a major trading, fishing and shipbuilding centre with a population of over 3,000. But like so many other settlements along the East Anglian coast, coastal erosion gradually took its toll and much of the town was lost to the sea. Dunwich once had eight churches and almost all had to be abandoned as the sea advanced inland. It is said that it is sometimes possible to hear the sound of church bells coming up from the depths of the sea on quiet nights. Today the village lies between the heath to the north and Minsmere to the south. It consists of a row of Victorian cottages, a church, a small museum and a ruined priory. The steep shingle banks fronting the settlement provide natural flood defences and help reduce the erosive power of the waves. Fishermen still launch their boats from the beach, as they have done traditionally for centuries. Two or three gravestones are all that mark the site of All Saints church, which was abandoned in the late 1700s but which only fell into the sea in the Edwardian period.

Dunwich Heath

Dunwich Heath is part of a plateau which once stretched from north Suffolk all the way to Ipswich. Known locally as the "Sandlings" it was created by man and grazing sheep, following the clearance of original woodland. It is now an ideal place for walkers and birdwatchers and parts of it are managed by the National Trust. Public access is very easy with several excellent walks radiating from Dunwich offering visitors insights into local history, geology and the diverse patchwork of habitats around the village, including access to the neighbouring bird reserve at Minsmere. Nearby Dingle Marshes are home to the rare and intriguing bittern, a large bird with a strange and haunting booming call. They are most often seen during May, and there are only around 20 pairs in England.

Saxtead Green windmill

Dating from 1776 this elegant and beautifully restored white windmill is a fine example of a traditional Suffolk post mill in full working order. Located approximately two miles north-west of Framlingham, the mill stands prominently in the surrounding flat countryside. Owned by English Heritage it is open to the public between April to October. There has been a post mill at Saxtead Green since 1287.

Framlingham Castle

Situated 18 miles north-east of Ipswich, Framlingham Castle is a magnificent landmark. The building has 13 towers linked by a curtain wall. Beautiful views of the reed-fringed mere and surrounding countryside and town can be enjoyed from the battlements. The castle has an intriguing and chequered history and over the years has been used as a fortress, an Elizabethan prison, a school and poorhouse. It was at Framlingham that Mary Tudor was proclaimed Queen following the death of her father Henry VIII.

Sizewell Beach

Sizewell Nuclear Power Station, owned by British Energy, dominates the Suffolk coast in this region. There are two power plants on the site – Sizewell A which was built in the 1960s and Sizewell B constructed between 1988 and 1995. For 10 years the two plants have supplied almost 3% of the UK's entire electricity needs, and Sizewell B is one of the largest employers in the county and the UK's only large pressurised water reactor. Sizewell A is in the process of being decommissioned. The colours of the station were carefully chosen so as to blend in with the environment by the Commission of Fine Arts.

Sternfield

The small village of Sternfield is mid-way between Saxmundham and Snape, approximately six miles inland from the delightful seaside towns of Aldeburgh and Thorpeness. The swans were photographed in February at the fishing lake at Marsh Farm Caravan Site, which has a secluded and peaceful location.

Suffolk Wildlife Trust has over 60 nature reserves and works hard to protect wildlife for the future. The county has 40 miles of heritage coast set in an area of outstanding natural beauty. Visitors can enjoy the rich and varied landscape, coastal resorts and gently rolling farmland.

Thorpeness

Situated two miles north of Aldeburgh on the Suffolk coast, the beautiful village of Thorpeness (below) was created as a model seaside village in the early 1900s by Scottish landowner and playwright G Stuart Ogilvie who bought the old fishing hamlet of Thorpe and turned it into a planned holiday village.

The postmill

The weatherboarded turret postmill, which sits on top of its matching roundhouse, was originally built in 1803 at nearby Aldringham as a corn mill, but later moved to Thorpeness in 1923 where it was converted into a water pump. Today the roundhouse is home to a local history collection. The metal-framed building seen in the distance is part water tower, part house; the house was incorporated into the design since locals thought that a plain water tower might be unsightly. It is now known as "The House in the Clouds", one of Suffolk's most famous follies.

Snape Maltings

Snape Maltings is a unique cluster of 19th-century malthouses and granaries nestling beside the river Alde five miles inland from Aldeburgh. The site houses the 800-seat world-class concert hall which hosts the famous annual Aldeburgh Music Festival. Other old buildings on the site are now galleries, shops and restaurants. A tragic fire destroyed the first concert hall in 1969 but it was rebuilt in time for the following year's festival. In 1979, the adjacent barley store was converted into the Britten-Pears School, commemorating composer Benjamin Bitten and his partner the singer Peter Pears. The nearby quay, built to accommodate barges bringing coal to the maltings and carrying malt to breweries, is now lined with pleasurecraft and boats offering pleasure trips down the river Alde.

Snape church

The church of St John the Baptist at Snape stands on high ground approximately one mile north of the village and a short walk from the Maltings. Originally the building was thatched. The nave was built in the 13th century and the tower and porch added in the 15th century. Inside the church there is one of the most

beautiful fonts in the county. The village sign (left) reflects the history of the village – from the Benedictine monks at the ancient Priory of St Mary to the curlew which symbolises the sources of inspiration of the composer Benjamin Britten who loved the sea, the marshes and the countryside around the river Alde.

Aldeburgh

The modern sculpture *Scallop* by artist Maggi Hambling is sited on the beach at Aldeburgh and is dedicated to Benjamin Britten. The composer found the area irresistible and made it his home; his opera *Peter Grimes* is based on the town and draws inspiration from a poem by Aldeburgh poet George Crabbe. Britten lived in The Red House in the village with his partner, the singer Peter Pears, from 1957 until their deaths in 1976 and 1986.

The seafront at Aldeburgh has changed little since Victorian times although it has often suffered from the encroaching North Sea. The distinctive 16th-century Moot Hall, on the seafront, now houses a small museum. The majestic 15th-century parish church of St Peter and St Paul's contains the grave of Benjamin Britten and the bust of George Crabbe, born in the town in 1794. Sadly Crabbe's house at Slaughden, close to the southern edge of Aldeburgh, has long been lost to the sea.

Orford

An unspoilt fishing and tourist village south of Aldeburgh, situated between Orford Ness, Tunstall Forest and Rendlesham Forest, Orford appears to have been little affected by the 21st century. The narrow streets and quaint fisherman's cottages look the same now as they did when they were built. Originally the settlement developed around the 12th century Royal Castle, and today the 90ft (27m) keep dominates the small town and its surroundings. The town was both politically and commercially important during the reign of Henry II, who built the castle between 1165 and 1173 to defend the area against seaborne invaders. Today, visitors come to the area to visit the keep and enjoy views from the top of the battlements, to explore Havergate Island Bird Sanctuary or to walk the large shingle spit of Orford Ness.

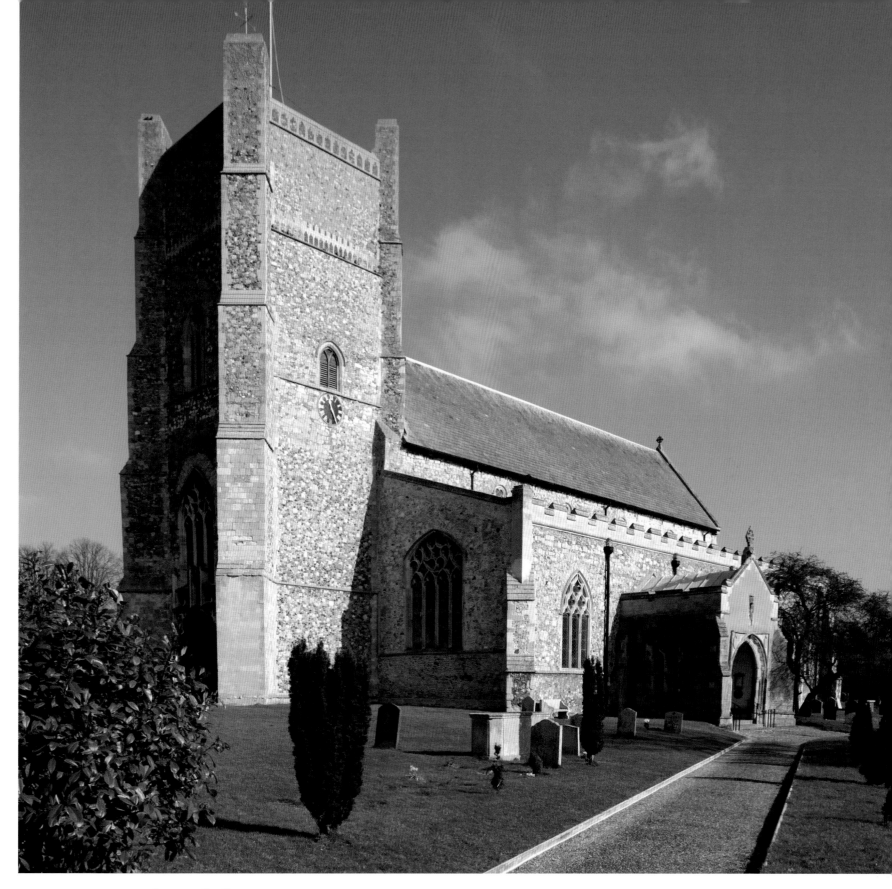

St Bartholomew

A few hundred years ago the estuary of the river Alde was just south of Aldeburgh. Over time, silting up of the river mouth diverted its path and created a spit between the river and sea stretching for over 10 miles down the coast towards Orford, enclosing the estuaries of both the river Alde and the river Ore. This has created a long stretch of sheltered water which is perfect for sailing and boating. The church at Orford dedicated to St Bartholomew the Apostle was largely rebuilt in the 14th century.

Lavenham

This beautiful medieval village which lies a few miles north-east of Sudbury is famous for its collection of half-timbered buildings. Lavenham was one of the wealthiest towns in Britain during the late middle ages

thanks to the prosperity of the local wool trade. The Guildhall of Corpus Christi (right) overlooks the market square and was established in 1592 by one of the three wool guilds set up in the town to regulate the industry. The lavish church of St Peter and St Paul (far right), which stands like a sentinel on a hilltop at one end of the high street, was rebuilt in the 15th century to celebrate the Tudor triumph at Bosworth Field. It has a 141ft (43m) tower – the tallest village church tower in Britain.

Felixstowe

Felixstowe is an attractive seaside resort and is Britain's largest container port. The town is well-known for its extensive and glorious gardens that run the length of the promenade and into the town centre. Along the seafront are the Spa Pavilion Theatre which features ballet, drama and pantomime, and a modern cinema.

At Felixstowe Ferry, which is part of the old town, there is a ferry across the estuary to Bawdsey where there are several well marked walks, which are popular with birdwatchers, and the local fish and chip shop has a well earned reputation for fine food. At the other end of the town, on the Languard Peninsula, there is an observation quay where visitors can watch the ships going in and out of the ports of Felixstowe and also Harwich, which lies across the estuary in Essex. Languard Fort just behind the observation quay is an ancient monument. Built in 1744 and modified in 1875 with further modern day improvements, tourists can visit this interesting building and learn about its fascinating history.

Felixstowe docks

Felixstowe is Britain's largest container port and the fourth largest in Europe after Rotterdam, Hamburg and Antwerp. The port recently welcomed the largest merchant ship in the world, the *Emma Maersk*, which docked at Felixstowe on its maiden voyage from China. The ship is a quarter of a mile long and as tall as a 20-storey building.

The owners of the town's beach huts (left) are clearly imaginative when it come to naming their prize possessions, and must be very fond of their tiny holiday homes.

Bedfordshire, Hertfordshire and Essex

The three counties north-east of London form a southern and western border to the heartland of East Anglia. Bedfordshire, with its southern border only 30 miles from London, is often referred to as the gateway to the Midlands and East Anglia. The old coaching road of the A1 connected London and Edinburgh. The villages along its route derived much of their wealth from this important link and they are graced with old staging inns and mellow brick buildings. The A1 also acted as a dividing line within Bedfordshire and Hertfordshire, with the area to the east becoming a natural part of eastern England. Much of northern Essex too, with its exquisite villages and stunning coastline, has characteristics in common with Suffolk, its northern neighbour. Constable Country straddles the two counties in the beautiful Dedham Vale.

Sandy

The attractive building and gardens, right, is the headquarters of the RSPB at Sandy. Formerly known as The Lodge, the building has an intriguing history. During the Second World War there was a fuel storage facility adjacent to the Lodge on the Potton Road. This was part of a national network of pipelines and tanks used to feed the multitude of wartime airfields in the region. Sometimes the fuel was used to clear away fog and mist, when a ring of fire would surround a landing strip and dissipate the damp air forming the fog, known in wartime parlance as "FIDO"! The site is still operational and now belongs to the pipeline agency. The RSPB is a charity with one million members, 170 nature reserves and 10 regional offices; the RSPB's main purpose is to work for a better environment rich in birds and wildlife.

Westmill

Between Stevenage and Bishop's Stortford, the pretty tree-lined village of Westmill has often been a winner of Hertfordshire Conservation Society's best kept village competition. It lies just off the historic Roman road of Ermine Street (now the A10), in the upper section of the Rib valley. The village is surrounded by arable farmland, pasture and meadows; its elegant centre contains buildings constructed from a mixture of thatch, clay and brick. The sloping village green is dominated by an unusual covered pump; the nearby cottages, built by Samuel Pilgrim in the early 1700s, are called Pilgrim's Row. The village is overlooked by the beautiful Anglo-Saxon church of St Mary the Virgin whose tower was restored in 2001; there is an excellent tea-room and a fine pub, the Sword Inn Hand (left), whose entrance is framed by two magnificent trees.

Cromer Windmill

Cromer Windmill is situated on the Stevenage to Buntingford road just north of Ardeley. It is the last surviving white weatherboarded post mill in the county and has a brick roundhouse. Dating from the 17th century, it was restored by the Hertfordshire Building Preservation Trust in 1997 with a grant of £50,000. Early windmills were supported by huge upright posts which is why they were called post mills. The main post rested on two cross posts which were buried in the ground. It was the miller's job to ensure that the sails faced the wind by swinging the whole building round the central post. He did this by pushing a large beam called a tail pole, attached to the back of the mill.

Audley End

Audley End House stands on the site of the former Benedictine monastery of Walden Abbey. It is an early 17th-century country mansion, and was first granted to Sir Thomas Audley in 1538 by Henry VIII. Thomas Audley's grandson Thomas, first Earl of Suffolk, rebuilt the mansion between 1610 and 1614. The house is now only about one third of its original size. During the middle ages, the

gardens and grounds around Audley End House were the cultivated estate of the abbey. In the 18th century the magnificent park was transformed from its formal design into one of "Capability" Brown's most stunning and successful pastoral landscapes. The parkland and Victorian gardens around the house have recently been restored and an artificial lake constructed, fed by the river Cam. The glorious setting of this house is captured here as the sun sets one evening in early August.

Essex village signs

There are few areas of Britain that have such a strong tradition of painted village signs than Essex and this is particularly true of the more rural areas in the north of the county. The signs which are often placed on the village green or in the centre of the village rather than its outskirts, depict key events in the history of the village. Sometimes notable buildings or attractions in the area are depicted and some of the larger town signs will also often incorporate their coat of arms. Signs for Dedham, Finchingfield and Felsted feature timber-framed houses, whereas signs at Little Bentley, Berden and Tilbury Juxta Clare have agricultural scenes representing the strong farming traditions in these localities.

Seen here are the signs for Helions Bumpstead (left) and Ridgewell (right above) in north-west Essex near the Suffolk border and White Colne (right below) in the Colne valley north-west of Colchester.

Finchingfield

Finchingfield is situated between Sible Hedingham and Thaxted on the Braintree to Saffron Walden road. William the Conqueror gave *Phincingfelda*, as it was then called, to Roger Bigod for his services during the invasion. This picture postcard village has a green, duckpond and a windmill, together with several medieval houses known as *cabbaches*. Many of the cottages have pargetting on their walls which is very characteristic of the area. The unusual tower of the beautiful church of St John (left) with its cupola looms over the village.

A popular stop for visitors, the Causeway Tea Cottage was built in 1490,

two years before Columbus discovered America. It is easy to see why Finchingfield is often described as the most photographed village in all of Essex.

The letterbox and telephone box (right) at Wimbish Green seem to be fighting a losing battle with the surrounding vegetation. This small rural village is just five miles from Saffron Walden.

Thaxted

The handsome town of Thaxted contains a famous Guildhall and winding streets lined with medieval houses which seem to lead towards the cathedral-like church of St John. Originally a town of thatchers, which gave the town its name, Thaxted subsequently became a centre of the cloth and cutlery trades. The name of the small hamlet of Cutler's Green, to the west of the town, harks back to Thaxted's heyday as a centre of cutlery manufacturing.

The conventional tower mill (above) was built in 1804 by John Webb, around the same time that the population of London was growing rapidly. Webb was a landowner, farmer and innkeeper. The bricks used in its construction came from his own brick and tileworks nearby. The walls are 4ft thick at the base and 18 inches thick at bin floor level. Towards the end of the 19th century it had become uneconomic and in 1904 it was closed down and its sails locked up. The mill now houses an agricultural museum which gives an insight into farming life before the days of mechanisation.

Morris dancing

Thaxted is the spiritual home of Morris dancing. The revival of this traditional pursuit was begun locally in 1911 by Mrs Miriam Noel, wife of the local vicar, Fr Conrad Noel. Today the Morris Men dance traditional Cotswold dances in Thaxted and its surrounding villages and towns between May and September. The annual gathering of Morris Men from all over England (above) is an amazing spectacle. It takes place on the first weekend following the spring bank holiday and draws crowds from all over the country. The high point of the festival is the dancing of the Abbots Bromley Horn Dance late in the evening when the town is packed with visitors.

The picturesque almshouses (left) are situated in the churchyard. These low thatched buildings were constructed as a priest's house which today is known as The Chantry. Dating from 1713 they have been immaculately restored to provide accommodation for three elderly couples. Thaxted has many medieval buildings, has changed little over the centuries, and is considered by many to be the jewel in the crown of Essex.

One of Thaxted's most famous residents was the composer Gustav Holst. His house can still be seen in Town Street, where he composed his most famous work, *The Planet Suite*.

Colchester

The capital of Roman Britain, Colchester is Britain's oldest recorded town. Its castle (far left) was constructed on the site of the Roman temple of Claudius by William the Conqueror in the same style as the White Tower in the Tower of London. Today it is an award-winning museum with many hands-on displays which illustrate Colchester's fascinating history from the Stone Age to the Civil War. Tymperleys Clock Museum (above) is housed in a 15th-century timber-framed building, once the home of William Gilberd, physician to Queen Elizabeth I. The beautiful clocks on display were made in Colchester between 1640-1860. The courtyard garden at Tymperleys is a welcome oasis of peace in the heart of the city.

Flatford

Flatford Mill lies at the heart of Constable country, in the Dedham Vale, on the river Stour in Suffolk. Constable's family owned the mill at Flatford and, as a boy, the painter spent a great deal of time there learning the family trade. Many of the buildings around the mill featured in Constable's idyllic pastoral paintings. Probably his most famous, *The Hay Wain*, depicts Willy Lott's cottage (above). Willy Lott was one of the mill-hands who worked for Constable's father at Flatford. The mill buildings are now owned by the National Trust.

Dedham

In the opinion of Nikolaus Pevsner, the distinguished architectural writer, Dedham "is easily the most attractive small town in Essex". The village is located on the Essex side of the river Stour, opposite Flatford, and it has many associations with Constable. Dedham Hall (right), a splendid Georgian building, now a private house, was once the Old Grammar School where Constable went to school. He lived close by in the village of East Bergholt and walked to Dedham every day to go to school. The High Street is the main thoroughfare with Mill Lane branching off to the mill stream and the river Stour. From the village it is a picturesque stroll of about a mile along the banks of the Stour to Flatford Mill.

The impressive parish church of St Mary, built with money provided by wealthy local cloth manufacturer Thomas Webbe, has dominated the centre of Dedham since 1492 and its stout square tower features in a number of Constable paintings. One of them, *The Ascension*, is on permanent display in the church.

Frinton

The North Essex coastal towns of Clacton, Frinton (left) and Walton all benefit from the clean sandy beach which extends from Jaywick to the south-west of Clacton to the Naze – a natural headland which protrudes into the North Sea. Frinton was developed as a planned seaside resort between 1890-1900. It was a fashionable place to visit between the two world wars, when the golf and tennis clubs were frequented by the international high society set; Connaught Avenue, the main entry to the seafront, became known as "the Bond Street of East Anglia".

Clacton

The one time sleepy fishing village of Clacton blossomed into a seaside resort in the late 19th century when Peter Schuyler Bruff, an engineer and manager of the Eastern Union Railway, built a pier which gave access to London by boat. He supervised the wooden pier's construction and it opened in 1871. It had an uninterrupted deck and very soon became a popular attraction for promenading and not just a place for landing goods and passengers. Pier improvements continued during the 20th century and the Ocean Theatre opened in 1928. Today Clacton is a lively resort at the heart of the "Essex Sunshine Coast".

Tollesbury

Tollesbury is often referred to as the village of the "Plough and Sail", because it relied on the harvest of both the land and the sea. It is an attractive village situated on the north bank of the Blackwater Estuary, between Maldon and West Mersea and

overlooks coastal marshlands. The settlement expanded rapidly in the late 19th and 20th centuries, and the countryside around the village (which is a conservation area) has changed constantly over the last two centuries, as the marshlands have been drained and embankments constructed. The restored wooden sail lofts (above) were used to store equipment for Edwardian racing yachts. At the centre of the village is The Square. On the west side stands the King's Head, the seafarers' pub; opposite is the church of St Mary the Virgin, dating from around 1090.

Maldon

This historic hill town stands at the head of the Blackwater Estuary and is home to many historic Thames sailing barges which can be seen regularly moored up by the Jolly Sailor Inn at the quay in Maldon. These boats were once the maritime workhorses of eastern England and were used to carry cargo, including hay, from the farmlands of Essex to London as feed and bedding for horses – they were often called "haystackers" due to the piles of hay on deck. The boats were built with flat bottoms so that they could rest up in the muddy creeks and inlets of the Essex coast at low tide. These days the graceful barges with their traditional tan sails earn their living carrying people on leisure trips.

The estuary has a well-earned reputation for wildlife. Vast numbers of birds are attracted to the area each year, where they take shelter through the winter. Thousands of ducks, wading birds and geese can be seen in the area. There are excellent walks on both sides of the Blackwater estuary starting from the town.

Mistley

North-east of Colchester, on the southern bank of the Stour estuary, lies Mistley, a picturesque village which adjoins the larger town of Manningtree. Mistley grew rapidly in the 18th century, thanks to local landowner Richard Rigby who wanted to turn the settlement into a spa town. He employed a number of prominent architects including Robert Adam but the plans collapsed when Rigby mismanaged his position as Paymaster of the Forces. Two of Adam's designs can still be seen: Mistley Towers, the unusual twin constructions designed to sit at either end of the new church of St Mary the Virgin (never built due to Rigby's financial collapse) and the Swan Basin in the High Street opposite the Thorn Hotel. Close to Dedham Vale, the town is a gateway to Constable Country.